doon wir way

A PHOTOGRAPHIC ARCHIVE OF CAITHNESS CHARACTERS AND EVENTS

PHOTOGRAPHERS:
Janet and Ian McDonald
and Bill Glander.

Published by:
North of Scotland Newspapers
Home of the
John O'Groat Journal
& Caithness Courier
42 Union Street, Wick, Caithness, Scotland.

CONTENTS

Doon Wir Way

A Photographic Archive of Caithness Characters and Events

THE PHOTOGRAPHERS

Janet and Ian McDonald

Bill Glander

A Catalogue Record for this book is available from The British Library.

Copyright © 2002 North of Scotland Newspapers

ALL RIGHTS RESERVED

Copyright © of the photographs in this book remains with J. McDonald, Photographers

ISBN 1 871704 30 8

Photocomposed by North of Scotland Newspapers, 42 Union Street, Wick, Caithness, Scotland.
Printed by Highland Printers, Henderson Road, Inverness, Scotland.

INTRODUCTION

"Doon Wir Way" is a photographic record of people and events gleaned from the archives of Wick photographers Ian and Janet McDonald and Janet's father, the late Bill Glander.

The business of J. McDonald Photographers, started by Ian in 1947 in Harbour Terrace, has been in full-time operation since 1950, when he returned from doing national service. He and Janet were married in 1963 and later moved their shop to Shore Lane, where they still live and work. The day to day running of their expanded business is now in the capable hands of their eldest son, also Ian. They realise that they have only skimmed the surface of what their cameras have recorded for over half a century and they are indebted to the public for their support and help with supplying names and information and they apologise for any errors caused by the memory playing tricks! They also thank Clive Richards of North of Scotland Newspapers, without whose perseverance and hard work, this publication would not be possible.

Bill Glander was born in India in 1903. He served in the RAF before and during the Second World War and was posted to Wick from the south of England to take charge of the Meteorological Office in 1947 for a two year posting. That two year posting lasted until his retiral in the early 1960s and he spent a very happy retirement in Wick until his death in 1980. His all-consuming hobby was photography and he spent hours in his darkroom making black and white prints and later colour transparencies, which he showed to appreciative audiences in and around Wick in the 1950s before the sophistication of television came to the north of Scotland. The camera he used to take most of the slides was a Vito B, requiring much more skill than today's automatic equivalents and although some of the slides deteriorated since they were taken in the 1950s and early 60s, their subject matter is important enough to include them in the small selection in this book. His daughter, Janet, still shows some of his slides of local shopkeepers and well-known people of that era and she says that her father would be proud to know, that what gave him so much pleasure, has become an important record in the history of the town, which he took to his heart and in which he and his family were made so welcome.

Ian and Janet would like to dedicate this book to their three grandchildren, Ross, Nadia and Siobhan and to all the young people in Caithness, who are our future.

Mr Willie Thomson, when being told off for parking, assured Sgt. William Mackay and Constable Donald William Munro that he wasn't parking – he was just pausing!

Down Memory Lane
with Bill Glander

The Hon. Robin Sinclair, Chief Constable Jack Georgeson and Sir Archibald Sinclair await the arrival of the Queen Mother at Wick Airport.

The Wick Pipe Band on parade for Remembrance Sunday.

Pipe Major Jim Christie of Wick Girls' Pipe Band, pictured behind his home in Louisburgh Street.

Pipe Major Donald (Dada) Davidson of the Wick Pipe Band.

Tossing the sheaves at a Young Farmers' Rally at Wick Riverside.

A Young Farmers' event at Wick Riverside, when contestants battled it out in the three legged race.

Ploughing the traditional way at Gillfield near Wick.

Paraffin oil was delivered to the fishing boats in Wick harbour for many years by Willie Taylor and his horse-drawn tanker.

Down Memory Lane with Bill Glander

A change of duty for Mr Willie Dunnett, engine driver, to Provost of the Royal Burgh of Wick.

Wick's first and only lady Provost, Miss Bessie Leith.

Baillie George Gunn of Wick Town Council.

Draper, Mr David Robertson, in his shop in High Street, which made way for the widening of the street beside Mowat Lane, Wick.

Another long serving member of the Wick library staff was Mr John Glass.

Long serving headmaster of Wick North School, Mr A. B. Henderson. Try doing those sums on the blackboard now!

County librarian, Dr. Fred Robertson.

A well known character was Mr Willie Thomson of Newton Hill, who had an illicit still somewhere near his home. Although it was common knowledge, he led the local constabulary a merry dance before the long arm of the law caught up with him and justice was meted out.

Miss Barbara Bain in her magical Aladdin's cave of an antique shop in Back Bridge Street, Wick

lizabeth McCrae, daughter of Wick medical practitioner, Dr R.H.B. McCrae, who was often seen helping at the Mart in Wick before she went to Agricultural College, subsequently married a farmer and now lives in Rothiemay.

Well-known and respected auctioneer, Mr Ben Sinclair, of Alexander Sinclair and Sons, pictured in his mart, with its public entrance off Bridge Street, Wick before he retired and sold it to Aberdeen and Northern Marts in 1962.

Cup of tea time at one of Bill Glander's popular slide shows in the country. Mrs Glander, who often accompanied her husband to the local village halls, is pictured in the background.

Sales of Work were a regular event in everyone's diary in Wick and Mrs Kenneth Duff-Dunbar of Hempriggs House is pictured making a purchase at one of the sales she opened.

A sight no longer seen – the Wick War Memorial with the Henderson Memorial Nursing Home bathed in winter sunshine.

The crew of the Golden Dawn, (back) Bobby Adamson, (left) Sanny Adamson and (front) Donnie Adamson and Alfie Mackay (right

John Sinclair (left) and Sandy Barnie on the Boy Peter.

Wick lifeboat being pulled up the slip into the lifeboat shed.
Second cox, John Sinclair, is visible in the stern of the boat.

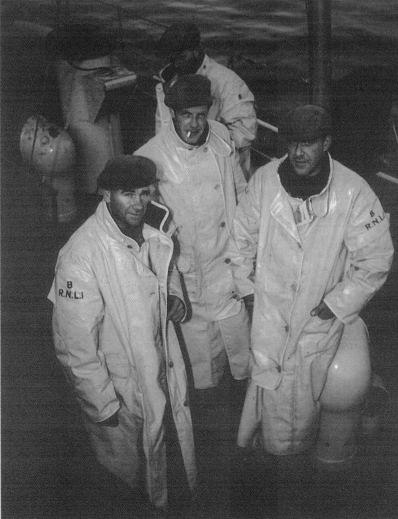

Among the crew of the Wick lifeboat
were (from left): Alfred Mackay,
James Mackay and Donnie Mackay.

Hand-written paperwork for Caithness-shire Chief Constable, Mr Jack Georgeson, in Wick Police Station.

Sergeant William Mackay, of the Caithness-shire Constabulary, affectionately nicknamed "Tiptoe", was a familiar figure in Wick.

Sergeant Swanson and his secretary, Norette Macpherson, in
the Civil Defence Office in Wick.

Inspector Neil Sutherland of
Caithness-shire Constabulary.

Saturday morning always saw the fishermen in the harbour preparing their nets for sea on the Monday morning. Sanny Adamson (rig and his brother Donnie, were pictured at work on the Golden Dawn. They used to take meteorological readings at sea, so Bill Gland (and his camera) was a regular visitor to the Golden Dawn each Saturday morning to retrieve the data.

Willie Dunnett, engine driver, ready to drive the steam train to Inverness.

full volume, the young girls of the Wick Girls' Pipe Band march smartly down Kirkhill from their base in Louisburgh Street, Wick.

Wick Girls' Pipe Band held practices at least twice a week and a full attendance was required, come what may!

Rev. Alistair A. Roy of Bridge Street Church, where he is still the minister.

Rev. Robert McGhee, minister of St. Andrew's Church, Wick.

Rev. R. R. Sinclair of the Free Presbyterian Church in Wick.

Rev. James Bews of the Wick Central Church.

Rev. John Robertson, minister of Wick St. Andrew's Church.

Rev. W. Nethercote Scott of Wick Old Parish Church.

Down Memory Lane with Bill Glander

A Remembrance Sunday parade, with the 1st Wick Company Boys' Brigade, led by their captain, Mr Willie McAllan (right) and Lt. Hamish Webster.

The Girls' Brigade marched smartly in the Remembrance Sunday procession to the War Memorial.

Long serving compositor on the "Groat" was Mr Norman Glass.

Sandy Cormack, checking the "Groat" as it rolled off the press in Union Street, Wick.

Down Memory Lane with Bill Glander

William G. Mowat in his shop, Mowat's Drapers in Bridge Street, a business originally owned and run by his father. Mr Mowat was Wicks' last Provost.

Mr George Mackenzie in his drapers shop in High Street, Wick. The building has been replaced and the site is now occupied by the Alliance and Leicester Building Society.

Mr Walter Sutherland, a benevolent chemist, who was "everyone's doctor" was much loved by his customers in Pulteney. The busine in Macarthur Street, Wick is still a chemist shop, Pulteneytown Pharmacy, now owned by Ian Smith.

High Street grocer Bill Henderson, whose shop is now occupied by George Mackay's butchers.

Mr Jimmy Miller, in his gent's outfitters shop at the narrow end of High Street, Wick now housing a mortgage shop.

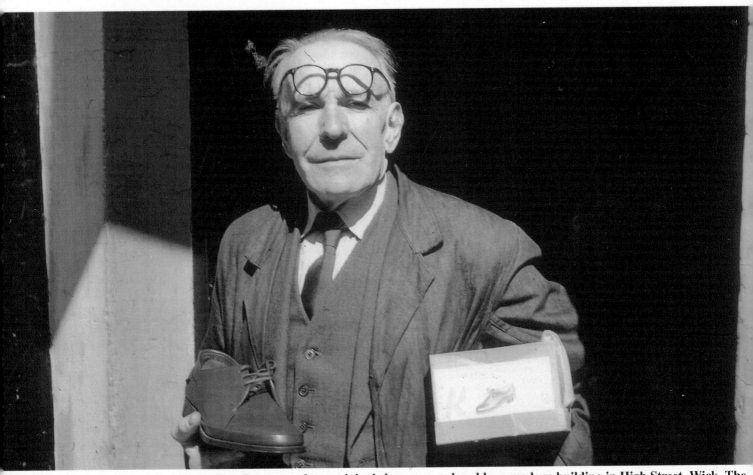

fine pair of shoes is offered for sale by Dan Dunnett, whose original shop was replaced by a modern building in High Street, Wick. The business was continued by his son, Graham, and is now occupied by the Highland Hospice charity shop.

Mr Jimmy Cuthbert, dispensing medicines in Boots the Chemist in Bridge Street, Wick, where he worked for many years.

John George Macleod in his newsagents shop in Bridge Street, Wick (now Young, Robertson & Co, Estate Agents).

alwarts of the Wick Boys' Brigade, Captain Sandy Hood and padre Rev. James Bews, pictured in the old BB Hall. The Boys' Brigade used to attend services in the West Church (now the site of Dunnet's Garage) and then the Central Church each Sunday.

...d by Captain Hood (on right), the 1st Wick Company of the Boys' Brigade paraded to the War Memorial on Remembrance Sunday.

The "father" of Caithness County Council, Mr Abrach Mackay, pictured leaving the Council offices.

After the "Kirking of the Council" ceremony in Wick Old Parish Church, Provost H. Leishman led the baillies and councillors back to the Town Hall.

Down Memory Lane with Bill Glander

Mrs Lily Christie at work making kilts and plaids for the pipers and drummers of the Wick Girls' Pipe Band. Lily was a second mother to all the girls on their many trips, all over the country, with the band.

An early picture of Wick Girls' Pipe Band taken at Kirkhill before a parade.

Headmaster of Pulteneytown Academy, Mr George Henderson, in the old school which is now the Assembly Rooms.

John E. Donaldson, the legendary journalist, "Hot News", was an accomplished musician as well as news gatherer.

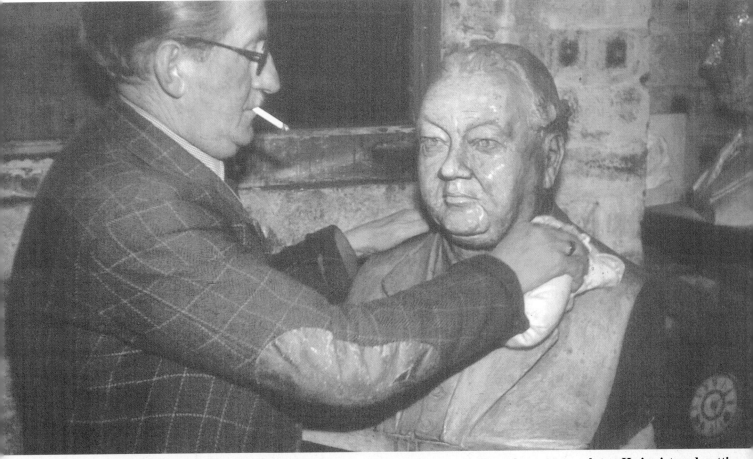

Mackenzie "M M" Miller had a draper's shop in Bridge Street, and was also a very talented amateur sculptor. He is pictured putting e finishing touches to the bust of Mr James Robertson, County Clerk of Caithness County Council. His shop is currently occupied by Graham Begg's toy shop.

Working in Bowles' Bakery in High Street are Jessie Stewart and Harry Bowles.

Mr James Robert Miller of W. & A. Geddes is pictured with a model of a piece of agricultural machinery.

Mr George Bain, manager for BEA in the Wick office in High Street, beside Woolworths.

Brigadier Sir Keith Murray, Convener of Caithness County Council, pictured awaiting the arrival of the Queen Mother on one of her early visits to the county.

Well known county councillor Mr John S. Banks, John O'Groats.

Enthusiastic bowler and manager of Fred Shearer's Gents' Outfitters on The Cliff, Mr David Gall, polishes his bowls as he relaxes at home.

"Cuba" Cormack, resting on the seat in High Street, Wick, on the way to his home at Kirkhill House.

Down Memory Lane with Bill Glander

Wick Songsters in the Salvation Army Hall.

ith the youth organisations stretching almost the full length of Bridge Street, the Wick Scouts, led by Mr A. Abernethy, paraded to the War Memorial.

Two civic leaders at the opening of the Caithness Central Hospital, Provost William Dunnett of Wick and Provost John Sinclair of Thurso, who was also Lord-Lieutenant of Caithness at the time.

VIP visitor to Wick airport, Mr Harold Macmillan, pictured being interviewed by Mr David Oag, long-serving editor of the "Groat" and freelance journalist, John Donaldson (right). On the left of the picture is Mr David Falconer and peeping through is Miss B. Simpson, Miller Avenue. On the extreme right of the picture is young Alison Banks, whose father had the drapery shop in High Street, Wick.

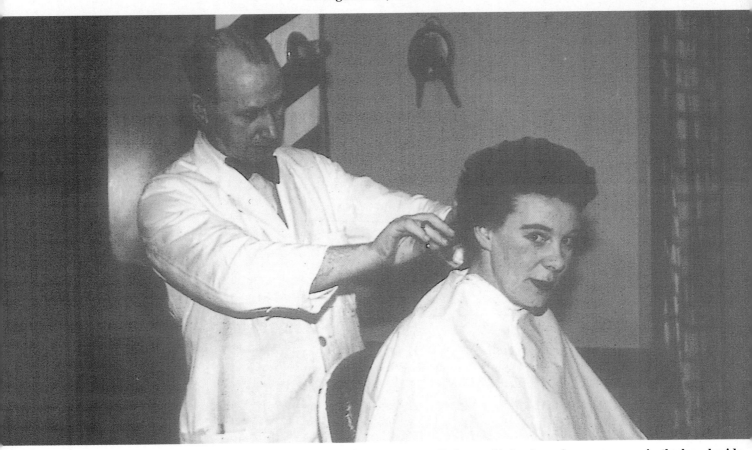

Mrs Nancy Eaton called in at Jimmy Bain the barber's for a quick trim. Jimmy Bain ran his business for many years in the lane beside Mowatt's drapers in Bridge Street.

Tucking in at the tea break, during one of the slide shows, this time in Tannach Hall. Pouring out the milk is Mr Willie Thomson from Newton Hill.

Another High Street draper, Mr Charlie Begg, outside his shop, which along with others, has been replaced by a modern building used by Boots the Chemists.

A tribute to the Queen Mother and family

charming study of the Queen Mother, as she sat among the profusion of flowers in her garden at the Castle of Mey, shortly after her 99th birthday.

After signing the visitors' book in Wick Town Hall, and still in mourning for the King, the Queen Mother paused to chat with Provost Miss Bessie Leith and town councillors outside the Town Hall.

With Commander and Lady Doris Vyner, the Queen Mother chatted to Princess Margaret, who was to fly south by helicopter, following a very early visit to Caithness.

A tribute to the Queen Mother and family

On her way to the Ship's Wheel antique shop, the Queen Mother casually strolled along the pavement in Thurso in the 1960s.

Princess Margaret often accompanied the Queen on the Royal Yacht, Britannia, when they called in at Scrabster to spend the day with the Queen Mother at the Castle of Mey. Princess Margaret was accompanied on this occasion by her children Lady Sarah Armstrong-Jones and Viscount Linley.

A happy picture of the Queen on an early visit to Scrabster en route to the Castle of Mey.

A tribute to the Queen Mother and family

The Queen Mother had a few words with some of the crowd who had gathered to watch her plant a tree at Wick Riverside during the town's quatercentenary celebrations in 1989.

Lady Fermoy's hat had already succumbed to the strong Caithness "breeze", but the Queen Mother managed to hang on to hers on their arrival at Wick Airport at the start of the annual summer holiday at the Castle of Mey.

1990 was a very successful year for the Queen Mother's pedigreed Aberdeen Angus cattle and North Country Cheviot sheep, as the ta[ble] laden with silverware in the Castle of Mey dining room shows. The Queen Mother is pictured with her factor, Martin Leslie (2nd rig[ht] farm manager Donald McCarthy (3rd left), his wife, Nancy, and their two sons, Danny and Sandy (right). Following Mr McCarthy'[s] sudden death, Longoe Farm is now run jointly by Danny and Sandy.

The members of the Canisbay and District Royal British Legion were greeted by the Queen Mother after they had held a special chur[ch] parade to Canisbay church on the 50th anniversary of VE and VJ days in 1995.

A tribute to the Queen Mother and family

A welcoming bunch of flowers from Lindsey Stewart when the Queen Mother arrived at Wick Airport for her summer visit to the Castle of Mey.

On her annual visit to Mey Games, the Queen Mother met some of the residents of Caberfeidh Court, Wick.

The Queen Mother enjoyed her favourite spot among the flowers in her garden at the Castle of Mey, when she returned to Caithness shortly after her 99th birthday. This is one of a series of photographs taken specially for the readers of the John O'Groat Journal and Caithness Courier, as a gesture of the Queen Mother's gratitude for the respectful way the people of Caithness welcomed her and respected her privacy, when she visited the county each year.

Prince Charles shared a joke with Mrs Chrissie Budge and Mrs Doris Sutherland when he visited the Laurandy Centre in Wick on a whistle-stop tour of Caithness.

Class Act

Just look what Santa gave us! Mrs Allan's nursery class in Pulteneytown Academy posed for a picture with their VIP visitor in 1979.

Every pupil at Thrumster School had a part in this lavish production of the traditional story at Christmas 1980.

54

Class Act

At a Parents' Day at Wick North School, the pupils of the two Primary 7 classes surprised their headmaster, Mr David Bruce, by formally presenting him with an inscribed pen stand to mark the fact that they were the first class to complete their primary education under his guidance, because Mr Bruce was appointed headmaster when they first started school in 1970. Front row (from left), David Steven, Heather Fraser and Linsey Murray, who also spoke on behalf of the pupils.

It was story time for Primary 2 of Wick South School, as the children gathered round their teacher, Miss Bobbie Veronda, who was on a year's exchange in 1985 with South School teacher, Miss Eleanor Leishman, from her school just north of San Francisco.

A photograph of Mrs Ronaldson and her class pictured at the North School's Christmas tree as the 1975 holidays drew near.

Sausages always taste better on sticks at a party, say the smiles on the faces of these under fives, who enjoyed the Jack and Jill Playgroup sessions during 1978.

1981. The pupils of Keiss School gathered in the school hall for a farewell presentation to Mr Allan Lannon, who had been their headmaster for four years. In those four years, Mr Lannon organised school trips to Edinburgh and York, a train journey from lmsdale, a boat trip to Orkney and a bus trip to Inverness. He supervised the school sports, introducing House Teams and held many fund raising events, culminating in a Grand Fayre. His production of the pantomime, Aladdin, in which the whole school took part, was a great success and being such a popular headmaster, everyone was sorry to see him go, but wished him every success in his new appointment as headmaster of Mount Pleasant School in Thurso. Mr Lannon received a scroll from Elaine Sutherland and hotographic equipment from Peter Richard. Mrs Lannon, who taught part time in Keiss, received a pendant from Dawn Goodfellow and their children, Fiona and Andrew, each received a book token.

ybster's senior citizens were treated to a grand night out in the Community Centre in 1981 by youngsters of the Lybster Youth Club, who are pictured with their guests after they had given each one a small gift.

For 20 weeks in 1981 Wick High School pupils learned the arts of First Aid from one of their teachers, Mr W. J. Miller (seated 3rd right) and 19 pupils were awarded the Junior Certificate of the St. Andrew's Ambulance Association. The certificates were presented by the examiner, Mrs E. Crum, to:- Amanda Bryan, Fiona Crockit, Katriona Duffy, Anne Dunnett, Kay Forbes, Caron Lindsay, Catriona MacDonald, Elizabeth MacDonald, Peta Message, Rhoda Sinclair, Fiona Urquhart, Susan Young, John Coleman, Steven Fray, Brian Grant, Scott Henderson, Trevor Izzett, Mark Manson. Unable to be present was George Ewing.

Primaries One and Two who attended Thrumster School in 1981 are pictured with their teacher, Miss Fiona Thomson. Pictured from left are Alexander Sinclair, Angus John Macaulay, Lynne Stewart, Jasmine More, Paul Oag, Craig Chisholm and David Campbell all of Primary One. James Bremner, Neil Robertson, Julie Sinclair, Sinclair Miller, Kristen MacLeod, James Mackay and Jayne Campbell of Primary One.

Hold the Front Page

"Read all about it!" The 'Groat goes colour in the Wick Gala!

Waiting to catch the judge's eye are these pretty contestants in the Wick Children's Fancy Dress Parade at the Braehead in 1976.

Ladies of the Wick Co-op Guild prepared their goods for sale on the stall at the Wick Gala Week Fayre in the Square in 1976.

Worzel Gummidge and Aunt Sally.

Alice in Wonderland characters smile for the camera at the Children's Fancy Dress Parade at the Braehead.

"Flower Power" at the Wick Gala.

Handcuffs and batons at the ready, this dubious pair of police "women" prepare to persuade the locals to part with their money on Gala night.

South Sea islanders have fun in the sun during a Wick Gala Week procession.

Vocal persuasion to part with the pennies, from a Gala Week float!

There was a tartan invasion in Wick, as these collectors persuaded the crowd to fill their collecting cans.

KING ARTHUR IS FEELING SAD
HE'S HAVING TO USE INCONTINENCE PADS
HE DOESN'T WANT HIS COURT TO KNOW A THING
OR HE'LL BE CARRIED OFF TO THE OF WING

THE TIMBURY UNIT HAS GONE DOWN THE DRAIN
CAITHNESS'S LOSS WILL BE THEIR GAIN
WE THINK WE HAVE FOILED THEIR PLOT
TO TURN IT INTO AN OFFICE BLOCK

IF YOU'RE FEELING SICK OR RATHER POOR
MERLIN THE MAGICIAN HAS GOT A CURE
HE'S GOT A MAGICAL POTION IF YOU'RE FEELING TENSE
HE CAN EVEN CURE YOUR INCONTINENCE

Medieval fun on a Wick Gala Week float!

Martini "girls" skated around with their collecting tins.

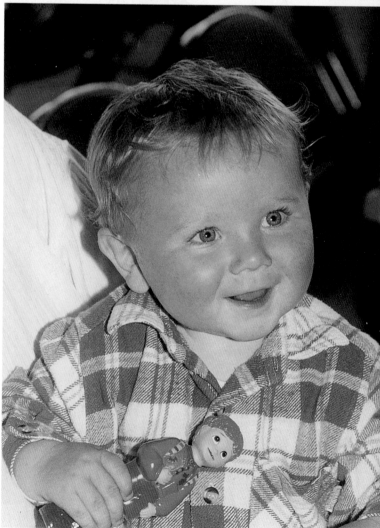

Plenty to smile about at the Wick
Baby Show.

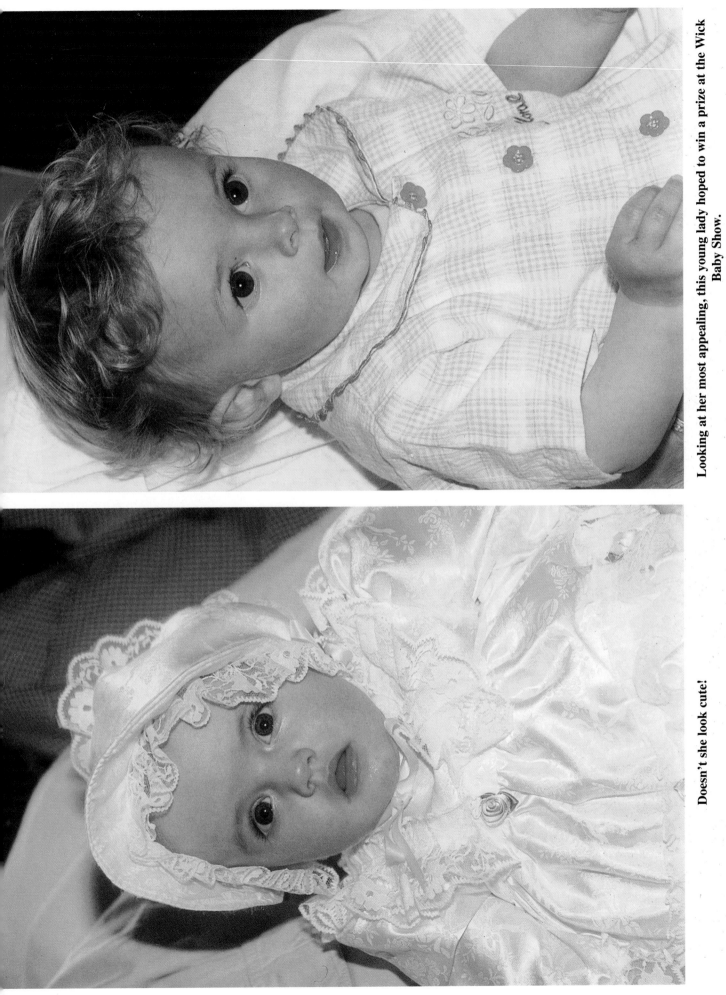

Looking at her most appealing, this young lady hoped to win a prize at the Wick Baby Show.

Doesn't she look cute!

The sign says it all!

"Like mother, like daughter" – captured at the Wick Baby Show.

World Cup "traveller".

Wick River Purification Board came under fire in this well decorated Gala Week float.

Claymore at the ready to fend off attackers!

Did these dusky maidens keep their "full of northern" promise?

"All at sea" during the Wick Gala.

With collection cans at the ready, Maisie Sutherland, an enthusiastic fancy dress collector of countless processions, was ready for the fun of the Wick Gala.

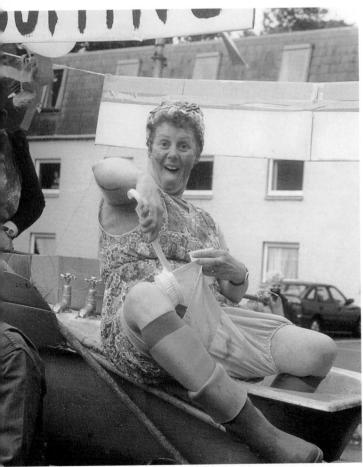

"Cleaning up the act" on one of the Wick Gala floats.

Off to "Emergency Ward 10", but collecting a substantial amount of money on the way, during the Wick Gala procession.

Clowning around at the Wick Gala.

Wartime matron from the 'Wick at War' float in the Gala Week Procession.

Power to the pram pushers! This overgrown baby brandished his own cotton bud as he collected money in his potty during a Wick Gala.

This Indian squaw found her way to Wick for the Gala Week procession.

These three dusky maidens used their considerable charms to persuade folk to part with their money during a Wick Gala Week procession.

"Mud, mud, glorious mud!" One of the Wick Gala Week collectors.

A very muddy County Show came under the spotlight on one of the Wick Gala Week floats.

Keith de Paola's Punch and Judy show was a popular attraction in the Assembly Rooms during one of Wick's Gala Weeks.

A "croft-hoose family" were in town for the night of a Wick Gala.

Batman and Robin at the Braehead Fancy Dress Parade.

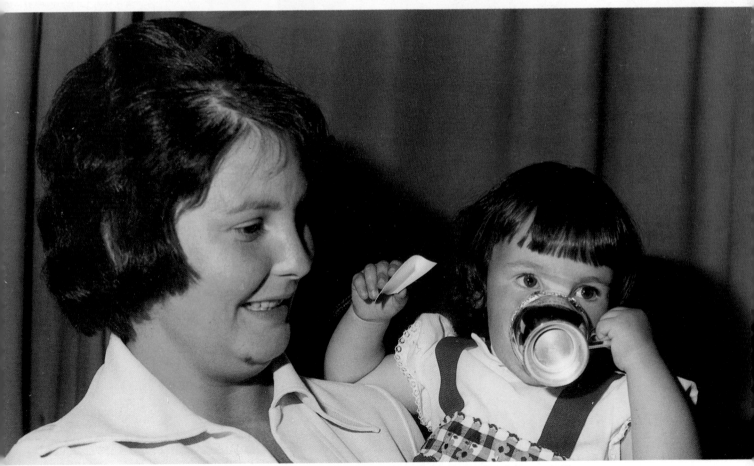

"They gave me this cup for winning the Wick Baby Show, but it's empty!"

FORGET THE WINE LAKE AND MOUNTAIN OF BEEF — IT'S PARTY TIME BY THE CORAL REEF

Catching coppers on the Coral Reef float.

These herring gutters from a bygone era came back to persuade the crowd to part with their money during the Wick Gala night procession.

Doon Wir Way

Who would resist this caveman collector?

The fancy dress collectors came in all shapes and sizes as they made their way through the crowds persuading them to part with their pennies.

Piracy on the high seas on a Gala Week float.

The "Domino Effect" was the theme of this Wick Gala Week float.

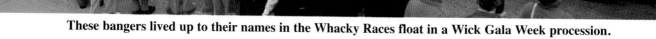

These bangers lived up to their names in the Whacky Races float in a Wick Gala Week procession.

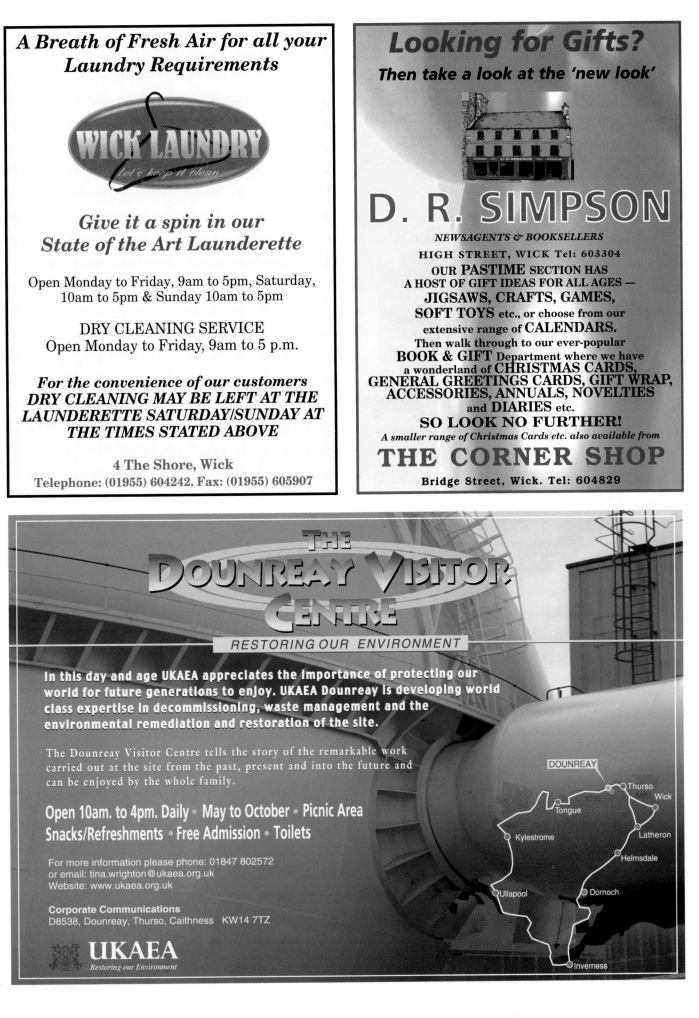

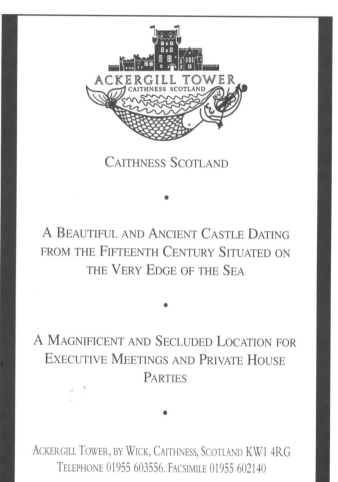

There's no business like show business

Best foot forward for the Cake Walk Competition for these pupils at the Elise Lyall School of Dance in 1995.

Making the toes tap away back in 1977 were the members of the Wick Scottish Dance Band. (L-R) Addie Harper, Robert Cameron, Hamish Auld, Isobel Harper and Eann Nicolson.

Ready to rehearse a sketch, with Daisy the Cow in the 1980 Gang Show, are the Wick Cubs who performed in the Assembly Rooms every second year from 1978 until 1984. The Gang Shows involved all the Cubs under the overall direction of Cub Leader, Mr Ian Mackenzie and their enthusiastic performances delighted the capacity audiences.

There's no business like show business

ick Old Parish Church held a Soiree in the church hall as part of the 50th anniversary of VE Day celebrations in the town. Thespians ready to perform are, from left, Mrs Nancy Durrand, Mrs Kathlyn Harper, Mrs Phyllis Gray and Mrs Dorothy Durrand.

The patients in the Queen Elizabeth Ward of the Caithness General Hospital were delighted when Robin Hood and his Merry Men in the guise of Rev. Alex Robertson (seated centre) his wife, Sister Kathleen Robertson, (left) and various members of staff, staged a mini-pantomime for them in December 1993.

Making their mark on the music scene in 1987 were "Fast Forward" comprising of, (from left) Lee Nightingale, Glen Campbell, Fiona Sutherland, Kevin Henderson and Gordon Mitchell.

Wick (RBLS) Pipe Band posed for a formal photograph outside the Pipe Band Hall in High Street in 1996.

There's no business like show business

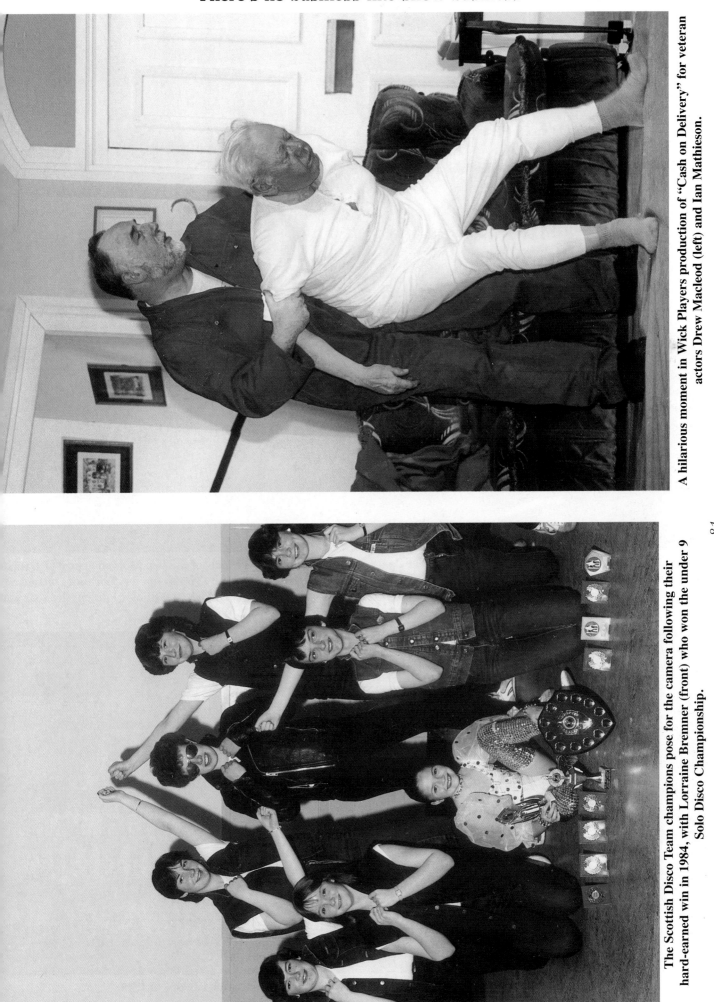

A hilarious moment in Wick Players production of "Cash on Delivery" for veteran actors Drew Macleod (left) and Ian Mathieson.

The **Scottish Disco Team** champions pose for the camera following their hard-earned win in 1984, with Lorraine Bremner (front) who won the under 9 Solo Disco Championship.

With more silverware to add to their collections, these four dancers were the Pupils of the Year of the Ben Morven School of Dancing, Wick in 1980. Senior winner was Brenda Mackay (right), New Cottage Farm, Howe, Lyth and runner-up was Barbara Oman (left), Janitor's House, Newton Road, Wick, Carina Campbell (2nd right), 78 Roseberry Terrace, Wick, was Junior Pupil of the Year and runner-up was Avril Ross (2nd left), 54 Leith Walk, Wick.

The dancers of the Elise Lyall School of Dance, pictured in the Assembly Rooms in 1999.

the request of his staff and friends, the Wick RBLS Pipe Band paraded at Dunbeath Castle in 1993 in a tribute to the owner and local benefactor, Mr R. Stanton Avery.

A lighter moment for the Wick RBLS Pipe Band in 1999, as they paraded in fancy dress, led by resplendent Drum Major Raymond MacDonald.

Caithness Junior Fiddlers prepare for a performance in the Assembly Rooms, Wick, in March, 1986.

A Wick Rotary Club fund-raising Cheese and Wine party in the Rosebank Hotel, in 1985, was livened up by this enthusiastic barber shop quartet comprising of (from left) Hugh Crum, David Morrison, Ronnie Bruce and Bill Mowat.

Mrs Elise Gill of the Elise Lyall School of Dance took over the old Sea Cadet Hall at the top of the Black Stairs and, with a lot of investment and hard work, turned it into a practice hall for her many pupils and into a home for herself and her husband, Martin. Elise is pictured putting some of the tots in the beginners class through their paces in the newly opened hall in 1996.

These youngsters thoroughly enjoyed the workshop held by the Scottish Ballet in the Assembly Rooms in June 1985.

A popular group, who sang at many functions in the 1970s, were the Melodymakers. (Back Row L - R): David Hill, Jim Grant, Bob Moyes, Alan Smurthwaite, Ronald McKain and Ian Burns. (Front Row L - R): Edna Morrison, Evelyn Kay, Margaret Wood, Liz Paul, Della Smith and Nancy O'Brien.

Well known faces in the Scottish music scene in 1985 were The Bobby Coghill Quartet – Ina Miller, David Smith, Christie Duncan and Bobby Coghill.

Doon Wir Way

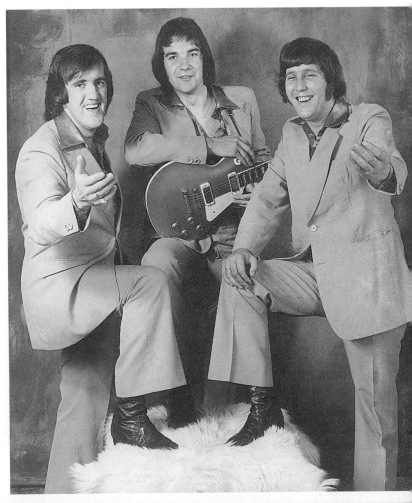

From the "swinging sixties" into the seventies, the Newmen – Stanley Macnab, Neil McConnachie and Willie Byrne were in the forefront of the Caithness music scene in 1971.

"Harmony" – Kate and Richard Bain and Jim Halliday were in great demand in 1985.

The famous "Scotland the What" team featuring comedians, Stephen Robertson (left), George Donald (centre) and Buff Hardy (righ relax after playing to a capacity audience in the Assembly Rooms, organised by the Rotary Club of Wick in 1992. Pictured with them rotarians Gerry O'Brien and Ronnie Fraser (2nd right).

The Wick Players' outstanding success in winning the Community Drama Association national finals was recognised at a civic receptio in Wick Town Hall in 1998. Caithness Area Convener, Councillor John M. Young (3rd right) presented a specially commissioned painting of the stage set by Pete Hodgson (2nd left) to Wick Players Chairman, Eric Farquhar (left), secretary/producer, Donald Farm and the main actors in the winning production, Andrew Craigie (centre), Kevin Farmer and Benny Douglas.

Christmas entertainment by Wick Players in 1980 was the Scots comedy "Cambusdonald Royal". The cast are picturd on stage in the
embly Rooms (from left) Frankie Farquhar (ghost of a monk), Jean Steele, Margaret Manson, Jenny Stewart, Marina MacDonald, Bill
ruce, Robert Manson, Raymond Durrand, John Green, Ian Mathieson, Andrew Craigie and (seated) Maureen Miller (left) and Susan
Levens.

rerunners of "Scotland the What" in Caithness in the 1950s were the Caithness County Architect, Mr Willie Wilson (left) and Medical
Officer of Health, Dr McCoubrey, who are seen entertaining the audience at the Caithness Agricultural Dinner in 1952.

A scene from the Wick Cubs Gang Show, which was staged in the Assembly Rooms in 1982.

90

By the left
quick march . . .

**The years ahead will tell us if this young enthusiast will become a fully fledged drummer in the
Wick RBLS Pipe Band.**

Brownie Revels in the Assembly Rooms in 1977, when Brownies from all over Caithness joined to enjoy an afternoon of fun and games.

By the left quick march . . .

Keiss Brownies celebrated their 10th anniversary in 1978.

Back home after an exhilarating weekend at Rumster in 1978, members of the 5th Wick Brownies are pictured outside St. Andrew's Church, where they met each week.

The members of the 1st Wick Ranger Guides gathered for a very special presentation to two of their members in 1980 – Lesley Swanson (standing 4th left), Thuster and Valerie Forbes (standing centre), Northfield Avenue, Wick, who received their Queen's Guide badges and certificates, presented by Lesley's sister, Fiona (standing 3rd right) who was a member of the Junior Council of the Girl Guide Association. Fiona was home on holiday from Aberdeen, where she was studying at Robert Gordon's. Ranger Challenge Certificates were presented to (front row left - right) Janet Swanson, Thuster, Ann Smith, Newton Avenue and Judy Reid, Kenneth Str both Wick. There are eight Queen's Guides in the picture, four of them the Swanson sisters from Thuster, whose mother Mrs J. Swanson (right) was District Commissioner for Wick South. Also in the picture is Ranger Guider, Mrs Katy Burns (2nd left).

A group of the 1st Wick Scouts, pictured with their leader Mr David More, in the Scout Hall in 1977.

By the left quick march . . .

A bit young to sign up perhaps, but this young lad enjoyed the thrill of sitting on one of the motor cycles used by the Highlanders during their recruiting drive at Wick Riverside in 1997.

Wick BB's and Lifeboys raised money during their 1987 session which they used to buy equipment for Wick Lifeboat and for the ambulance.

A rousing send-off at Wick Rifle Hall, for Company Sgt. Major William Davidson, 40 Seaforth Avenue, who retired in 1971 after twenty years' service with B (QOH) Coy, 2/51 Highland Volunteers.

3rd Battalion of the 51st Highland Volunteers pictured in 1978 outside the Rifle Hall, Wick, following an inspection by G.O.C. Scotland Lt. General Sir David Scott-Brown (standing 5th right).

For those in need

Melt in the mouth cakes and freshly baked pancakes were quickly snapped up at the Papigoe and Staxigoe Playing Fields Association Sale of Work, which was officially opened by Mr Robert Maclennan MP, in 1976.

Even in 1977, the young folk of the town were raising money for an indoor swimming pool, and these youngsters from the Caithness Pop Club are pictured handing over a donation to Councillor Anderson Murray from the Swimming Pool Committee.

1983 was the 50th anniversary of Wick Players and one of the events to mark the milestone was a sponsored Bed Race from the Bignold Hospital to the Town and County Hospital by the Junior Players. The traffic ground to a halt in the town and they collected £219 from members of the public, which was included in the total of £500 raised. The money was used towards the purchase of a MECABED for use in the geriatric unit, which was of great benefit to both the patients and the staff.

The Wick committee of the Save the Children Fund are pictured in 1979, hard at work preparing for their 14th annual Thrift Shop which was held in the old Bank of Scotland premises, by kind permission of the Aberdeen Savings Bank. As usual the public had been very generous in their support and one splendid donation of a quantity of wool, single bed size blankets were to be sold at the bargain price of £5.00 each. Pictured at the arduous task of sorting and pricing are (left - right): Mrs P. Weir, Mrs R. McIvor, Mrs M. Lamont Mrs J. Sutherland, Mrs E. Crum, Mrs Lyall, committee chairman, Mrs J. Lapwood and Mrs Hood.

This Sporting Life . . .

East End Boys' Club under 10s pictured in 1977.

Hanging on to his every word, young footballers from the East End Boys' club, were privileged to have a coaching session with the Scotland team coach, Craig Brown (left), in 1996.

The Wick Academy football team pictured in 1980, proudly displaying the silverware gleaned during the season.

This Sporting Life . . .

Pictured with their trophies are the Wick Rangers football team in 1977.

The pupils of Hillhead School sported a strong United under 10s team in 1976.

The happy line-up of lads who successfully played for the East End under 14s team in 1978.

Raising money to finance their club activities, these lads of the East End Boys' club attempted the impossible by remaining silent for t
hours, in a sponsored Hush-in in 1978

The veteran's trophy was presented to Mr Alex Crowe by Mrs W. Miller at Wick Golf Club in 1977.

The East End Boys' Club Players of the Year trophies were presented to (from left) under 10s – William Mackay, 12 Robertson Square, Wick, under 12s – Kevin Farmer, 10 Wellington Street, Wick, under 14s – William Munro, 6 Robertson Square, Wick and under 16s – James Coghill, 12 Kinnaird Street, Wick by Mrs Mary Sinclair, whose late husband Bill devoted more than forty years to East End.

Lined up on a cold December day in 1980, are the teams from the Rosebank Hotel (left) and Mackays Hotel, who played an annual charity match to raise money for the Wick Senior Citizens' Treat. Refereed by Mr James Bremner, the result was a resounding win for the Rosebank Hotel, who made up for the previous year's defeat by winning 7 goals to 1.

1981 saw the 50th anniversary of the Rosebank Bowling Club in Wick. Club president's wife, Mrs Isobel Sinclair, 17 Brown Place, is pictured throwing the first jack to open the season, watched by the enthusiastic members who planned to hold special tournaments to mark their anniversary.

Having spent the winter bowling in the Assembly Rooms, these winning members of the Wick Indoor Bowling Club proudly display their trophies in 1983.

All things bright and beautiful

With Father O. Martin these youngsters took their first communion in St. Joachim's Church, Wick, in 1977. (From left) Adrian Kelly, Julie Dickson, Heather Robertson, Margaret Brown, Barbara Cabrelli, Helena Paterson and Patrick Cavanagh.

The ladies of Wick Old Parish Church, who distributed the monthly church magazine, pictured in 1981, with Mr John Cormack, the elder responsible for magazines. (Front row left - right) Miss Katy Banks, Mrs J. McBeath, Mrs N. Doull, Mrs Sutherland, Mrs Lough. (Middle row left - right) Mrs M. Manson, Mrs M. Anderson, Mrs R. Sutherland, Mrs I. Gates, Mrs C. Reid, Mrs A. Macphers (Back rows from left) Mrs S. Anderson, Mrs S. Miller, Mrs A. MacAllan, Mrs M. Munro, Mrs J. Shearer, Mrs F. White, Mrs P. Gra Miss M. Grant, Mrs I. Shearer and Mrs Gunn.

The congregation of Bruan Church held a special centenary service in July 1985.

All things bright and beautiful

ers of the Wick Central Church pictured after their Harvest Thanksgiving service in 1989 with organist, Miss Emma Bruce (from left)
Mr Wilfred Budge, Mr Fred McBoyle, Mr Robert Morgan, Mr William Miller, Mr Benny Grant and Mr John Swanson. The church
later closed and was bought by the Wick Baptist Church, whose own premises in Union Street needed major repairs.

a recognition of their dedicated service to St. John's Church over many years, Mr and Mrs Jack Banks (seated 2nd and 4th right) and
Mrs Peggy Walton (seated 3rd right) received gifts from the members of the congregation, who are pictured with their rector,
Archdeacon John Hadfield and Mrs Hadfield (seated left) in the church hall in Moray Street, Wick.

HY 140
HY 549
HY 176
HY 180
HY 191

HY 140
HY 549
HY 176
HY 180
HY 191

Christmas is always an exciting time for children and these youngsters learned the true story of Christmas by acting in a traditional nativity play in the church in 1977.

Amanda Gray of Louisburgh Street gave gifts to Captain Hamish Moore and his wife Sheena, after he had officially opened the Wick Old Parish Church Sale of Work in the Assembly Rooms in October 1977. Although he had been away from Wick for many years, Captain Moore's links with the Parish Church, where his father Rev. Gordon Moore had been a much respected minister, were renewed when he returned to take up the post of Wick harbourmaster.

Following major internal structural alterations to Wick Old Parish Church, which resulted in the congregation using their church hall across the road for Sunday Services for some considerable time, the minister, Rev. Stewart Frizzell, and elder, Mr William Harper, ceremoniously carried the bible, and led the congregation back into the church for the first service on Sunday 8th May, 1994. The alterations, which attracted a lot of opposition at the time, were met with almost unanimous approval from local people and visitors, including the Queen Mother, who found the church "very welcoming".

For long and dedicated service to St. Andrew's Church, Wick, elders, Mr Alec Campbell (left) and Mr John Duchart received long service awards and certificates from the minister Rev. Sandy Gunn. Their wives received bouquets at the special ceremony in the church in 1969.

Sunday school children from Wick Old Parish Church delighted the congregation with their Nativity play during the Christmas service in the Church in 1977.

We will remember them

He didn't really remember anything about the war, but this youngster was out to watch the VE 50th anniversary parade in Wick, in May 1995, complete with his union jack.

Would these youngsters be free to wave their flags, had it not been for the sacrifice made by their grandparents in the Second World War? These Girl Guides lined up in Bridge Street, Wick to honour the veterans, who paraded to the War Memorial for the service to mark the 50th anniversary of VE Day in 1995.

Wick Scouts and Cubs joined the masses who thronged Wick town centre to cheer the veterans from the Second World War.

We will remember them

mark the 50th anniversary of VJ Day in 1995, a drumhead service was held at Wick Riverside in the presence of the Queen Mother.

At the service, the Queen Mother met veterans of the Burma Campaign.

They served their country during the Second World War, and despite being in poor health, these three veterans were determined to take part in the parade to mark the 50th anniversary of VE Day.

To spontaneous applause, these veterans of World War Two marched through the town to the War Memorial for a service to commemorate the 50th anniversary of VE Day in 1945.

We will remember them

ined up at the War Memorial are some of the World War Two veterans, who attended a special service to mark the 50th anniversary of VE day in May 1995.

With each campaign medal representing an important slice of their lives, these veterans of the Second World War paraded through Wick on the 50th anniversary of VE Day in May 1995. Following a service at the War Memorial, they marched to the Assembly Rooms, where a lavish tea was laid on for them and their immediate families. What stories must have been exchanged that afternoon! Marching with the aid of a stick was former sergeant in the 5th Seaforths, Mr John More, Argyle Square, who also won the Military Medal during the war.

Well done!

Members of the Caithness Riding Club show off their trophies, won during the previous season, at their dinner dance in the Roseban Hotel, Wick in 1981.

Well done!

sentations from their colleagues and businesses in Wick, were made to two drivers from National Carriers, who were made redundant
the ending of the parcel deliveries by British Rail in 1981. William Gunn, Whitehouse Park, who was a loader, handed over the gifts
to Mr George Sutherland, Station House, Lybster, who had been 12 years with National Carriers and to Mr David Bremner
nd left front), Raggra, Thrumster, who had been employed by them for more than seven years. The presentations were made at Wick
station when the two drivers had returned on the train after delivering their lorries to Inverness.

Retiring in 1976 after many years' service as attendant at the Junior Occupational Centre at Wick North School, Mrs Jessie Gordon
(front centre), Newton Road, Wick, received a watch and a bouquet from her colleagues and parents at the Centre. The gifts were
presented by Miss Evelyn Webster (centre left) at a buffet in the Mercury Motor Inn.

Members of Latheron WRI with one of the trophies they won at the County Show in Wick in 1966. (From left), Mrs W. Forbes, Mrs J. Mackenzie, Mrs J. Shearer, Mrs W. Bull, Mrs J. Chisholm.

Senior Enrolled Nurse Jane Davidson (5th left), 1D Seaforth Avenue, Wick, retired in 1981 after nursing in the Town and County Hospital for ten years. Her colleagues held a special dinner for her in the Station Hotel, where Sister Bruce presented her with a gold watch and crystal vase from all the hospital staff and auxiliary nurse, Heather Sutherland, (3rd left) handed over a bouquet.

Well done!

There was a scary selection of witches, ghosts and things that go bump in the night, as well as more decorative costumes when these children enjoyed a Hallowe'en party in Staxigoe Hall in 1977.

119

Elise Lyall, 50 Seaforth Avenue, Wick, is pictured receiving the 1980 Pupil of the Year Award, for the third year in succession, from Jeanette Shearer. Runner-up for the second year was Robyn McBoyle, Rosemount, East Banks, Wick. Elise had a particularly good year, having won the cup for the Open National Dancing (this was the first time since the cup was award in 1949, that it had ever been north of Perth) and the cup for the Best Dancer in the Northern Counties, at the Edinburgh International Festival of Dancing Pre-championships. Robyn and her sister Diana (middle row, 3rd L) also won cups at the Pre-championships in Edinburgh. The successful young dancers were pictured with their fellow pupils of the Jeanette Shearer School of Dancing.

120

Well done!

etiring in 1981 after more than seventeen years as an auxiliary nurse in the now demolished Henderson Memorial Hospital and the
tral Hospital, Mrs Grace Nicol (seated 2nd left), 27 Glamis Road, Wick, received gifts from her colleagues, which were presented at a
cial dinner in the Queen's Hotel. The gifts, which included a pair of pictures by Douglas West and pieces of china, were handed over
senior nursing officer, Mike Cooper, (seated centre) and by Mrs Barbara Gunn (seated left), Wellington Avenue, a former colleague
in the Henderson.

llowing a career in the post office, which began as a telegram boy when he left school, Mr Robert Sutherland (seated 3rd left), postal
executive at Wick, was promoted to postmaster at Saltcoats. Gifts of a nest of tables and radio cassette player and bouquet to Mrs
Sutherland, were presented from his colleagues by Mr George Gunn (seated left) and Miss Sheila More (2nd left).

1981 Wick High School head boy, Gordon Carter, accompanied by rector, Mr John Macleod, visited the Adult Training Centre (now the Wellington Centre) to present a cheque for almost £55, which was the amount of the collection at the school's Easter service in the Central Church. Centre manager, Miss Elsa Macdonald, accepted the cheque on behalf of the trainees, who were allowed to stop work for the ceremony. The money was for the purchase of sports equipment.

Mr John Bruce (front 2nd left), Lochside, Sarclet, thought he was going to the 1985 Thrumster Rifle Club's annual dinner dance in Mackay's Hotel, Wick, but the event had been organised to honour him with a surprise presentation in recognition and thanks for the thirty years he had been secretary/treasurer of the club.

Well done!

Once again the air in the Assembly Rooms was heady with the scent of the beautiful blooms entered in the East Caithness WRI Bulb Show in 1979. Trophy winners and Bulb Show committee members are pictured with Mr and Mrs J. A.H. Macleod (seated centre) who opened the show. Back Row (left - right) Mrs B. Robertson, Thrumster (committee member), secretary/treasurer, Mrs G. Lyon, Berriedale, Mrs A. Miller, Killimster (best 3 hyacinths), Mrs P. Coghill, Killimster (best exhibit and best 4 daffodils), Mrs N. Brims, Killimster (winning Institute with under 25 members), Mrs H. Steven, Watten (committee). Front Row (left -right) Convener, Mrs M. Bain, Keiss, Lucy Calder (7) North Road, Wick, who presented a gift to Mr Macleod, Mrs M. MacGregor, Mid-Clyth, vice-convener and Mrs E. McCallum, Federation President.

Members of the Wick Model Yacht Club proudly displayed their trophies at their annual dinner dance in 1976.

The finals of the Central League of the Caithness Small Bore Rifle Association were held in the Drill Hall, Castletown early in 1981 with the winning team coming from Watten. Winners and office bearers are pictured (standing L - R) D. Morrison, Castletown (junior champion), David Bremner, Watten, Mrs Jean MacDonald, Watten (secretary of the County Association), H.A. Ross, Watten, D. Oliphant, Lyth (retiring president of the Central League), William Leitch, Canisbay (League Treasurer), George Gunn (president), A. MacDonald, Watten, Mrs B. Mackay, Watten, Adam Ross, Watten and John Bremner, Watten. Seated in front are the members of the Tait family, Dunnet, who won the Junior Team championship.

It was the pleasant duty for Wick Town Improvements Committee member, Mr William Mowatt, to present cheques to the youth organisations in the town, at a meeting in the Mowat Room of the Assembly Rooms in 1985.

Well done!

Trophy time for Wick RBLS Pipe Band juniors in 1986. Their trophies had been presented by Mrs Margaret Mackenzie (centre).

The residents of Berriedale, Dunbeath and Latheron thought so highly of Mrs Pat Anderson, their district nurse for over 12 years, that they organised a public collection and presentation to her, when she moved with her husband and family to live in Wick in 1979. Held in the Inver Guest House, Dunbeath, the gifts of a music centre and cheque were handed over to Mrs Anderson by Miss I. McIvor (right) watched by (from left), Mrs G. Lyon, Berriedale, Mrs M. Mackenzie and Mrs G. Gunn, Dunbeath.

Wick Choral Society interrupted one of their rehearsals in St. John's Church hall in 1978 to present cheques to Achvarasdal Eventide Home, which was accepted by Rev. W. Wallace (centre) and to Mrs Sheena Miller for Cancer Research. Mr Ronnie Bruce made the presentation on behalf of his fellow members.

There was a good entry in the annual Caithness Ornithological and Fur Society Show in the Assembly Rooms, where the trophy winners are pictured in 1977.

Well done!

wo former members of the Wick Telephone Exchange, who had each served 38 years on the night staff, received the Imperial Service Medal. Miss Mary Anderson, 16 Northcote Street and Mr W. H. Simons, 18 Kinnaird Street, are pictured after they had received the awards from Mr J. Currie (right), deputy manager from Aberdeen, at a ceremony in the Telephone Exchange in 1977.

trophy for well-known farmer Mr William Ronaldson, Westerseat, was presented by Mrs Bruce, whose husband Jim was president of the Caithness Agricultural Society. The presentation was made at the Society's annual dinner in the Portland Arms Hotel in 1962.

Mrs Jessie Doull, George Street, received the Wick Rotary Club Citizen of the Year Award in 1985, for all her voluntary work, most of which was quietly behind the scenes and not known about by the general public. A specially inscribed Bible was presented to her by Club president Rev. A. A. Roy. Mrs Doull was accompanied by her husband Arthur. Mrs Doull was later to become the overall winner of the Caithness Civic Awards in 2001.

Following her sterling work in organising the Wick Quatercentenary celebrations in 1989, it was fitting that Deputy Chief Executive, Mrs Jess M. Campbell should receive the Rotary Club of Wick Citizen of the Year award. The suitably engraved Caithness Glass bowl was presented to Mrs Campbell, who was accompanied by her husband, James (centre), by President Mr Peter Cadman at the Club's Christmas dinner in Mackay's Hotel.

Well done!

5 was a very successful year in the various Scottish events for members of the Caithness Riding Club, who won the Kiltarlity Jumping Cup and Stirlingshire Saddlery Cup. Proudly holding the Kiltarlity Cup are (front from left), Lynsey Bain, Elaine Harper and June mpbell. The Stirlingshire Saddlery Cup for a Quiz for Scotland was won by Bridget Holt (left) and Toots Bain. William Mitchell, Liz xander and Erica Jefferies were unable to be present when the photograph was taken at the Riding Club's dinner dance in Mackay's Hotel, Wick.

e young folk who enjoyed their sessions with Riding for the Disabled at Halkirk, were delighted when Mr Andrew Grant, president of e Rotary Club of Wick, visited them in 1992 to formally hand over a horse donated by the Club and they insisted that he had the first ride on the animal.

A very generous gift of bookcases from the family of the late Mr and Mrs Victor Fraser, George Street, formally presented by their daughter, Mrs Moira Gunn, was greatly appreciated by the residents of Caberfeidh Court. The bookcases were accepted by chairman of the Caberfeidh Court residents association, Mr W. G. Mowat.

Mrs Isobel Cuthbert, Newton Avenue, Wick (3rd right) whose talent at making dried flower pictures raised hundreds of pounds for charity over the years, on this occasion donated her profits to Spina Bifida Association in 1994.

Well done!

Billy Sutherland, the salesman from Sloans in High Street, Wick retired in 1978. The previous year he had a miraculous escape after being trapped in a snowdrift at the Ord for three days. He had survived by keeping himself warm by wrapping himself in ladies nylon tights he was carrying in his van. He is pictured (seated 2nd left) with the rest of the shop staff.

Lucky for some! Winners of Air Ecosse flights to Aberdeen, where they attended a recording of the Johnnie Beattie Show, Mrs Linda Munro and Mr George Moodie (2nd left) were welcomed on board by Air Ecosse deputy chief stewardess, Miss Gill Sutherland. Accompanying the winners were Miss Isobel Mackay and Mrs Munro's husband Thomas, and there to see them safely on their way was Air Ecosse manager at Wick, Mr Tony Johns.

After 19 years as a Club Steward, Mr Jack Mowat (seated 3rd left), 38A Dunnett Avenue, Wick, received gifts from the Caithness Cl
which were handed over by former president, Dr Charles Minto (seated 2nd right). Other members seated were (from left) Mr Georg
Meiklejohn, Mr David Sutherland, Club president Mr Christie Sutherland and Mr Harold Banks.

Following an article and photographs about the Wick Heritage Centre in a 1981 edition of the Caithness Courier, the Wick Society received a very unusual gift in the form of a very old parchment, dated 1476, detailing the return of certain lands to his father, Lord Sinclair, by his son, Oliver Sinclair. The donor was Mrs M. F. Coxon, Inverness, who had received a copy of the article from her niece, Dr E. Finlayson, East Greenland. The parchment had been found among the papers of her late uncle, Mr Alexander C. Mackay, who retired to Helmsdale where he died in 1947, having been rector of Falkirk High School from 1899 to 1924. The parchment had been translated and authenticated in Edinburgh and seemed to be part of an enormous rearrangement of his affairs undertaken in 1476 by the Earl of Caithness and although Oliver had to give back the lands, among which were Kirk, Noss and Landhallow, he was given, in return, all the Sinclair lands south of the Tay. Mrs Coxin (right) is pictured with Miss Nancy Roloff, secretary of the Wick Society, who accepted the parchment on their behalf.

Well done!

A stalwart member of the Save the Children Fund, Mrs Nan Graham of Northcote Street, spent many hours baking and making tablet for sale in their annual Thrift Shops. When her baking was sold out in the mornings, she hurried home to refill the empty tins, which helped attract more customers to support the worthy cause.

"Tea for Two" or "Tea for Two Hundred"? William (Sonny) and Bunty Bain had their magnificent collection of teapots on display in the Assembly Rooms in 1981, for a Caithness Federation WRI annual meeting. Sonny had begun the collection fourteen years previously, going to auction sales and carefully selecting teapots from beautiful antique china ones to the humble brown earthenware variety. At their home at 31A Dempster Street, Wick, there were a few treasured ones on display, with the rest carefully packed away, so it was the first time all the teapots had been on display together. The collection was greatly admired by the WRI members.

One man's fight against cancer led to a cheque for £928.50 being presented to Cancer Research in 1981. Alec John Bain (2nd right), 6 C View Place, Lybster, decided to do a sponsored walk from John O'Groats to Lybster, despite having had a major operation and weeks treatment in hospitals in Inverness. His motives were simple – if he could complete such a marathon, which to him was every bit as difficult as an End to End trek, then it might encourage other cancer sufferers to shake off their despair and begin to fight back to tr to lead as normal a life as possible again. Doctors advised Alec to do the walk in two or three stages, but with a willing band of supporters, including Lybster district councillor Peter Sutherland (2nd left) and Elaine Sinclair (right) who acted as treasurer, he walk the 30 miles in 9 hours 27 minutes. There was a large gathering of his friends and family in the Commercial Hotel, Lybster to see Ale hand over the cheque to Dr Stewart (left) who said that the money would be used to buy some form of cancer scanning equipment for in Caithness.

The oldest resident of the village of Thrumster in 1981 was 97 year old Miss Williamina Gunn, 17 The Crescent, who is pictured with Lady Jessamine Harmsworth, who was a regular visitor to her home. Miss Gunn, who was born at Brownabin, above the Quarry, ha seen a lot of change to the area in her long life and at the time, reckoned she was at least 20 years older than anyone else in the district When she was eighty, she spent four months in Canada, but failing eyesight was beginning to keep her indoors.

Well done!

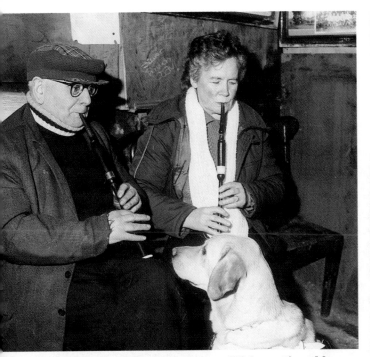

When Mrs Ella Glen, 4 Henrietta Court, Wick, continued her chanter and bagpipe practices with Pipe Major Jim Christie of the Wick Girls' Pipe Band, her guide dog, Eliza, was delighted to go with her, because the two sons of the couple, who trained her for the Guide Dogs for the Blind Association, both played the pipes. She used to sit enthralled in the old bakehouse in Louisburgh Street, while Ella and Jim practised. Ella's late father, Pipe Major Donald "Dada" Davidson of the Wick Pipe Band, originally taught Jim to play the pipes.

A 90th birthday cake and gift was presented, in 1994, to Mrs Jeannie Bremner, 21 Barrogill Street, from Captain Grace Gordon at the Wick Salvation Army Home League, which still meets every Monday afternoon. Also in the picture is Mrs Bremner's daughter, Mrs Mary Glass (right), who is secretary of the Home League.

Not too impressed with the importance of the occasion, eight week old Kerry Miller, Stewart Crescent, Thrumster, slept soundly in the arms of her great-great-grandmother, Mrs Bella Sutherland, Gersa. The other family members, pictured in 1986, who made up the five generations, were Kerry's great-grandmother Mrs Isobel Gunn, Maryburgh, grandmother, Mrs Sybil Mackay (standing right), Brickigoe, Thrumster and her mother Alice.

Wick Indoor Bowling Club Singles Champion in 1995 was fourteen year old Keith Campbell from Argyle Square, Wick. His mother, Janice, had just completed her very first season on the indoor rink, but she joined her husband Alan among the winners to receive trophies.

The Countess of Caithness and her young son, the Earl of Caithness, pictured at their ancestral seat of Sinclair and Girnigoe Castle in the summer of 1966.

The Quatercentenary year in 1989, celebrating 400 years of the Royal Burgh of Wick included a "Boundary Walk", which was enjoyed a large crowd of people who enjoyed the sunshine as they made their way round the harbour on a Sunday afternoon in April.

Well done!

At 96 years old in 1976, John Sutherland (left), Thornhill, Dumfries, was reckoned to be one of the "Groat's" oldest readers. Twenty-five years before, Mr Sutherland had farmed at Dunnet and Ardross, before retiring to Dumfries-shire. He was pictured arriving at Wick Airport, having flown unaccompanied from Edinburgh, to spend a holiday with his son William. An experienced traveller, Mr Sutherland had used most forms of transport, including the stage coach!

In the summer of 1981, Caithness's most dedicated member of the "rucksack brigade", David Begg, whose parents lived at Ledard, Robertson Crescent, Keiss, was off on his travels again. A keen photographer and writer, David's travels this time would take him to the land of the Midnight Sun, the North Cape and he planned to stay in Oslo with a couple he had met at the Thurso Folk Festival. David's travelling first began when he qualified from Jordanhill and he worked for a year as a labourer/teacher with the Frontier College in the far north of Canada, working in mining camps and also spending a period teaching the Cree Indians. From there he went to a kibbutz in Israel for three months before returning to Paisley where he got a job as an ice cream man! Denmark was his next port of call and he worked there for nine months as a spray painter. Meanwhile, his family had moved north to Keiss where they had relatives; his cousin is the famous wildlife artist Frank Begg and his father took up an appointment in Wick High School. David joined them for a short while before his travelling urge got the better of him again and he packed his rucksack and set off for Australia and New Zealand. He hitch-hiked across Australia and in New Zealand, a country he liked very much, he worked as a freelance writer and photographer for an educational journal and also set up a bicycle business for a friend, which gave him enough money to hitch-hike his way home through Asia and Russia. He found this a fantastic experience and took hundreds of slides, a small selection of which he showed to various organisations, including the Rotary Club of Wick, who were able to share some of the excitement of his journeying through Indonesia, Thailand, Burma, India and Nepal. David's photography showed the people, their work and their ways of life in their own environment and because he lived with them, rather than observing them as a tourist, he gave his audiences an evening to remember.

A chance meeting on Bridge Street, Wick, with Sir Gerald Nabarro for local bus driver, Mr Willie Mowat in 1970. Sir Gerald heralded the start of personalised car number plates. His car boasted the registration NAB 1.

Out of an entry of around ninety in the Poultry section of th 1981 Wick Fur and Feather Show, a Black Minorca bantam hen, belonging to eleven year old Evan Bain, 31A Dempster Street, won seven trophies. Evan had eight hens and three cocks entered in the Show and the three cocks and six of the hens were awarded places. Evan was no stranger to success with his poultry, as the mother of the winning bantam won trophies for him at the previous year's County Show.

The staff of Graham Dunnett's shoe shop, pictured with Major Dunnett (right) and Mr Mervyn Hockey from Clarks shoes, after Mrs Muriel Matheson (centre back) had received a television set, awarded by Clarks in a competition in 1976. Other staff members were (back row) Sylvia Polson (left) and Linda Bain and (front) Vera Orbell (left) and Caroline Duncan.

Well done!

pite very stormy weather, a large number of Wick's senior citizens attended the 1981 annual Treat, organised for them in the Assembly Rooms by the Wick Community Council. In his welcome, Council chairman, Mr W. G. Mowat, read a telegram from MP Robert acLennan and paid special tribute to Ian Ross of Anderson Drive, who had personally raised one third of the £390 donated from the charity football match between Mackay's Hotel and the Rosebank Hotel for the Treat.

It was not a case of "Keeping up with the Joneses in Wick bowling circles but "Keeping up with the Smiths", particularly the Smith family from Newton Avenue, who are all members of the St. Fergus Bowling Club. Son, Kevin, topped the poll by not only winning the Club Champion, but also winning the Champion of Champions award. Daughter, Anne, was Junior champion and also won the Gala Week Pairs. Father, Ian, won the Handicap trophy and shared the Pairs award. Skipped by father, the whole family won the Turner Cup.

The tablefull of trophies was presented at the club's dinner dance in Mackay's Hotel in 1976.

As the sun went down over Wick River in 1995, members of the Wick Rotary Club donned wellie boots and rubber gloves to clear some of the litter from the river bed.

Having a Ball

Nursing staff took time-off to enjoy themselves at the Hospital Dance in Mackay's Hotel in 1978.

Pictured at the Wick Quatercentenary Ball in the Assembly Rooms in 1989 were Ruth and Denny Swanson (left) and Alex and Doris Matheson.

School friends who attended the 50s Wick High School reunion in the Waterfront in the summer of 1993 were (from left), Sheila Miller, Anne Dunnett, Margaret Grant, Norman Miller, Stewart Sinclair, Ronnie Fraser, Andrew Mowat, Duncan Muir, Gina McAllan and Mona Smith

Having a Ball

"Ooh, la, la"! Wick Ladies Circle were in the mood for a French Night in the Mercury Motor Inn in 1983.

Enjoying a Christmas night out in the Norseman Hotel, Wick in 1980, are the staff of Ray Holt Drainage Ltd., Thurso.

The staff of the Cliff Bakery held a night out in the Mercury Motor Inn in 1977. (Back row l - r), Willie Swanson, Donnie Anderson Ray Yellop, James Sutherland and Brian Yellop. (Front Row l - r), Grace Henderson, Maureen Yellop, Claire Cornwall, Betty Yellop Doreen Macleod and Olive Durrand.

Keen golfers pictured at the Wick Golf Club dance, held in the Station Hotel in 1971 were (from left) John and Rona Farquhar, Alec and Nancy Miller, Donnie and Isobel Shearer, Ron and Pat Oliver, Clair and Nancy Manson, Billy and Ray Richard.

Having a Ball

Staff of the GPO and their friends enjoyed a dance in Mackay's Hotel in 1966.

A popular annual event was the Drivers' Dance, which took place in the Rosebank Hotel in 1972.

Members and helpers of the Wick Red Cross Disabled Club enjoyed a night out in the Mercury Hotel at Christmas 1977.

This group was pictured at the Building Trades Federation dance in the Mercury Motor Inn in 1977.

A New Millennium

The smiles and hats say it all, as these young folk joined the throng of revellers in the Market Square to welcome in the New Year and the new century.

147

Hats of all description were on display as folk gathered in Wick Market Square to say goodbye to 1999 and welcome the 21st centur

From tots to teenagers, everyone enjoyed the special family atmosphere.

148

Two thousand people thronged into the Market Square in Wick to welcome the year 2000. Families gathered from all over, the music played – even the weather was good as flares and fireworks heralded the 21st century.

At midnight on December 31st, 1999, the sky around Wick erupted as fireworks of all descriptions heralded the new millennium.

Oot 'n' Aboot

"Just a wee suck of the thumb, PLEASE!". A fun picture taken at the first Animal Day in the Market Square.

Lady Jessamine Harmsworth was the hostess for this gathering of the members of the MS Society, who gathered in Thrumster Hous to hand over their fund-raising cheque in 1981.

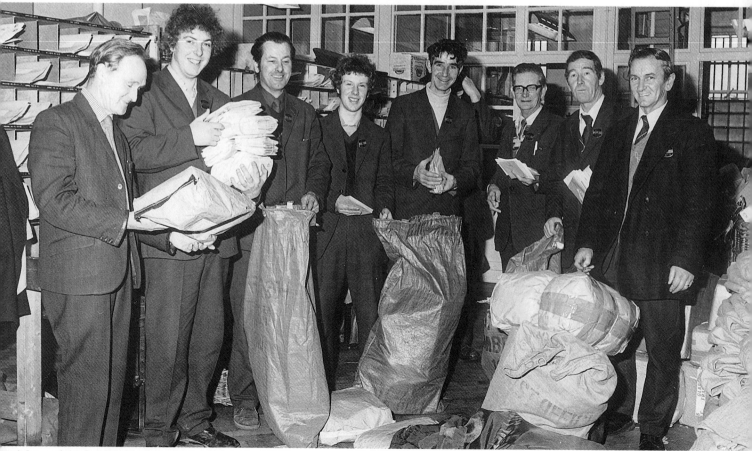

A busy time for the postmen in the Wick Post Office sorting office as they coped with mountains of parcels and cards in the run up to Christmas 1980.

The ladies of the Wick Luncheon Club enjoyed a day out on the train from Wick station in the summer of 1981.

The teachers who took part in the North School fancy dress netball tournament were cheered on by their pupils.

The opening of the Riverside Caravan Club Site at Wick in 1981 was performed by Caithness District Council Convener, Mr John You
The six and a half acre site, overlooking Wick River, has been a great tourist asset to the area. Guests at the opening ceremony were
Caithness District Council Chief Executive Mr A. Beattie (seated centre), Deputy Chief Executive Mrs Jess Campbell, chairman of th
Highland Centre of the Caravan Club, Mr and Mrs I. MacGowan, Inverness (3rd and 4th right) and Mrs Rona Taylor, Wick (5th rig)
whose late husband was an enthusiastic and hard working member of the Highland Centre.

A sunny day for Reiss Razamataz, although it doesn't seem to be very warm judging by the sweaters. Was it knobbly knees or a shape
legs competition, or a bit of both?

The Caithness and Sutherland heats of the 1978 Miss Highland Contest attracted a large entry. The finalists are pictured in Rosebank Hotel, where the judging took place and the attractive line up is (from left) – winner Ginny Wilson, Brora, Roselyn Miller, Wick (2nd), Drag McPhee, Halkirk, Caroline Munro, Bettyhill (3rd), Janice Miller, Castletown, Fiona Henderson, Wick, Margaret Steven, Barrock, Kirstin McIntosh, Wick, Elizabeth Robertson, Halkirk, Anne McGee, Wick and Marina Macdonald, Castletown.

Donkeys, sombreros and cases full of dirty washing returned to Wick with the members of Wick Youth club who had enjoyed a holiday in Spain in 1977.

One of the many useful projects tackled under the Jobs Creation Scheme in Caithness in 1977 was the insulation of lofts in council houses. Left - right: George Stewart, Martin Campbell and Mary McPhee.

In 1981, the well-stocked shop in the village of Thrumster was run by Mrs Marion Oag (right) and her assistant, Mrs Sheena Heppel.

Lorna Simpson and David Richard-Jones from the Development Department dressed up for the occasion at one of the first events in Wick's Market Square, following the pedestrianisation.

"I'll never finish that!". Scene at one of the successful events in the Wick Market Square in 1999.

On duty in the kitchen, these volunteers had the mammoth task of providing a hot meal for around 300 pensioners at the annual Senior Citizens' Treat in the Assembly Rooms, Wick and they still managed a smile!

The hall rang with happy chatter, as the pensioners waited expectantly for the meal to be served.

Feeding time at the Farm Animal Day in the Wick Market Square in 1999.

Medal winning gymnasts, who attended after-school classes in Wick North School in 1995.

The crew of the Wick Fire Brigade pictured at a roll call in the 1970s.

Haste ye back

The final meeting of the Caithness District Council was held in Wick Town Hall on March 18th, 1996.